Flying in Cornwall

Pete London

▲ In the 1920s and 30s, Percival Phillips' Cornwall Aviation Company used Avro 504K biplanes in alarming exhibitions of barnstorming, across the Duchy and beyond (AUTHOR'S COLLECTION).

◀ **During the First** World War, Women's Royal Naval Service personnel worked with male ground staff at Newlyn's seaplane base. The lady wears loose cotton overalls while she helps service the Short 184 floatplane behind (AUTHOR'S COLLECTION).

Published by Tor Mark, United Downs Ind Est, St Day, Redruth, Cornwall TR16 5HY

First published 2011 © Pete London 2011:

ISBN 978 085025 425 9

Designed by Alix Wood,
www.alixwood.co.uk

Printed by R Booth Ltd, The Praze, Penryn, Cornwall TR10 8AA

Front cover: Scillonia Airways' de Havilland DH.84 G-AHAG *Bryher* provided a passenger service between Land's End and St Mary's, principal island of the Isles of Scilly, between 1967 and 1969. Here, seen over Land's End, she's understandably been given markings proclaiming 'Scenic Flights' (AUTHOR'S COLLECTION).

Back cover: Jetstream T.2 XX476 61/CU of 750 Squadron based at Royal Naval Air Station Culdrose, on Cornwall's Lizard peninsula. The aeroplane is passing over the spectacular scenery of St Michael's Mount, near Penzance (AUTHOR'S COLLECTION).

Pioneers

A viation arrived in Cornwall during the long hot summer of 1910, when pioneer aviator Claude Grahame-White, one of the real 'magnificent men', brought his frail Farman biplane to the Duchy for some exhibition flights at Penzance. As his base he used a field named Poniou Meadow, just east of the town. During the evening of Saturday 23 July Grahame-White made the first aeroplane flight from Cornish soil, passing above hundreds of astonished local people gathered at the field to watch. He travelled over the town and on landing, received huge cheers from the wildly-excited crowd; no-one had ever seen anything like it. Grahame-White's later flights took him over the British fleets anchored in the shelter of Mount's Bay, before he returned home to London.

Following Grahame-White's excursion, it was 1912 before another flyer visited Cornwall; in mid June the French pilot Henri Salmet appeared with his Blériot monoplane. Salmet was sponsored by the Daily Mail to visit towns and villages throughout Cornwall, stir up public imagination and of course, promote the newspaper. He called at Bude, Lawhitton and Bodmin, and then pressed on to Newquay, Truro and Falmouth, where he landed near Budock's workhouse.

▲ **Cornwall's first ever** aeroplane flight, Saturday 23 July 1910; Claude Grahame-White and his Farman take off from Poniou Meadow, near Penzance. On the horizon, Paul village church can just be made out. The photographer's name, Vaughan T Paul, is in the bottom right-hand corner (Reg Watkiss).

Salmet then took a leisurely route home, via St Austell, Fowey and Liskeard. In 1912 too, the first Cornishman qualified as a pilot when Lieutenant R B Kitson, from Lanreath, gained Aviator's Certificate number 365 on 12 November, flying a Bristol.

During September 1913 Gustav Hamel arrived, another of the most prominent early aviators, British despite his name. Hamel's route took him over Padstow and Portreath before he headed south-west, and at Penzance he gave demonstration flights on his Blériot single-seater before big crowds. Hamel's ambition was to be the first man to fly to the Land's End and that he achieved on 24 September, taking off from Trengwainton near Penzance at 5.30 pm, and returning later that evening.

Of course, the early exhibition flights were incredibly popular and in April 1914 Henri Salmet returned to Cornwall with a two-seat Blériot, visiting Fowey and arriving at Falmouth on St George's Day. Again he was sponsored by the Daily Mail and the Blériot was decorated with an underwing title to that effect. Salmet circled over Falmouth to attract all the attention he could, but his landing on Gyllyngvase Beach was marred by the nose-over he performed in the soft sand there, in front of the crowd that had duly gathered. Fortunately, the damage to pilot and aeroplane was slight.

Falmouth's lady Mayoress, Mrs Chard, was keen to try the new-fangled means of transport, and Salmet agreed to fly her to Penzance. Overnight the

▲ **Gustav Hamel prepares** to get away on his Blériot monoplane during his visit to Penzance in September 1913. Helpers are ready to hold the aeroplane steady while the pilot tests his engine prior to take-off (AUTHOR'S COLLECTION).

▲ **Frenchman Henri Salmet** photographed with local dignitaries at Falmouth's Gyllyngvase Beach on 27 April 1914. He stands beneath the engine of his Blériot; the Lady Mayoress, Mrs Chard, is to his right (RCPS Research Project).

aircraft was repaired and fitted with floats, and on the morning of Monday 27 April the two made a start from the beach. Unfortunately, near Porthoustock the Blériot's engine failed and Salmet alighted off St Keverne. The aeroplane drifted, watched with awe-struck gazes by local children playing on the beach. Fortunately the tug Marion (Captain Mitchell) arrived, and towed the two aviators around a choppy Lizard Point into Mount's Bay; the Blériot was beached at Penzance. After that episode Salmet made several exhibition flights from the town, including trips over St Buryan and St Just. The next day he left for Barnstaple, passing over Newquay and Bude *en route*.

June 1914 saw the arrival of the first aeroplane at Redruth, when the Irish peer Lord John Carbery brought his 80 hp Morane two-seat monoplane down for demonstration and passenger flights. Over the three-day event the aircraft used a field belonging to Mr Sims' farm at Sinns Barton, just north of the town. Admission to watch the flying was one shilling (5p) although hundreds of people loitered for free by the edge of the field, a trait noticeable at air shows ever after.

During the good weather which briefly emerged on 25 June Lord Carbery gave flights to Miss Holman of the prominent Camborne family, and then her brother; he flew over Porthtowan, Portreath and Redruth itself. The following day Carbery demonstrated upside-down flying as well as several loops; the upper surfaces of the Morane's wings were marked with roundels to help the crowds make out the attitude of the aeroplane. During the day, Carbery passed over Redruth's town clock, Illogan, Portreath, Chacewater, St Day and Carnmarth. Sadly, Saturday witnessed thick mist but some brief flights were made, before pilot and aircraft travelled back east across the Tamar.

▲ **Lord John Carbery** with his Morane monoplane, seen at Sinns Barton Farm near Redruth during June 1914. The aeroplane bears the number 12 from a previous air-race (PADDY BRADLEY).

The First World War

During the summer of 1914, people all across Europe waited with dwindling hope for a halt in the slide toward war, but on 4 August German forces crossed the Belgian frontier. By autumn the ports of Ostende and Zeebrugge had fallen, and the Imperial German Navy increased its U-boat presence in the English Channel. Since Britain depended on the mass import of food and raw materials to live, let alone fight, and since all supplies came by sea, the potential of Germany's submarines to affect the war was acute.

Among other measures, the grave situation led to the formation of a network of airship stations around much of Britain's shoreline, under the control of the Royal Naval Air Service. Airships were ideal for lengthy aerial patrols in search of marauding U-boats; they could carry bombs, and stay aloft for many hours. Like many parts of the coast, the waters off Cornwall's long shores became witness to a grim battle between the airships and their underwater enemies.

The Lizard peninsula, pushing into the Channel, was a strategically important location for an airship base. During June 1916 Royal Naval Air Station Mullion was commissioned, on land belonging to the Bonython estate near the village of Cury, north-east of Mullion itself. The station became the centre of wartime airship operations in Cornwall. Its first airship was transported there by train; huge twin-engined Coastal Class C.9, which first flew from the new base on 18 June 1916 and began patrols on 1 July.

During 1916 Mullion acquired more Coastals; a total of five served there. Several smaller sub-stations were established subordinate to Mullion, which allowed patrols over wider areas with the available airships, and helped ensure air cover should the main site be closed due to bad weather. The sub-stations were built at Langford Barton just south of Bude, and also at Laira (Plymouth, Devon), Toller (Bridport, Dorset) and later Upton (Poole, Dorset).

◄ The enormous Coastal Class airship C.9 at Royal Naval Air Station Mullion, photographed during late 1916. Of the airships that served in Cornwall, C.9 was the most successful aggressor. In the background is a second C Class (J M Bruce/G S Leslie Collection)

The strength of the airship patrols was their powerful deterrent value. Fear of discovery made the U-boat captains wary of surfacing to recharge the batteries which powered their submarines' electric motors; this in turn reduced the raiders' effectiveness. Of the airships based at Mullion the most famous remained its first, Coastal Class 9, which became known as 'the darling of the Airship Service'. During an outstanding career C.9 was involved in many incidents, including the bombing of at least four U-boats, under her daring captain Flt Lieut J G Struthers.

Mullion also operated smaller Submarine Scout Zero Class airships; a total of ten served there between July 1917 and December 1918. But the SSZ was powered by only one engine, which on long patrols was something of a chancy business in terms of reliability. To circumvent the risk, during early 1918 a modified SSZ Class appeared, designed and built at Mullion by a group of officers under Flt Lt R S Montagu: the Mullion Twin. The new craft, at first designated the MT-1, became known as the SSE.2 ('E' for 'Experimental') and also acquired the rather grandiose local nickname Silver Queen. It was powered by two Rolls-Royce Hawk engines positioned one each side of its crew gondola, and first flew on 4 March 1918. The Mullion Twin was a successful design, and participated in many convoy escorts over the Channel.

▲ **Cornwall's own airship,** the Mullion Twin, designed there by a group of Royal Naval Air Service officers during 1918, underway at her home station. A large team of ratings manhandles her across the airfield (AUTHOR'S COLLECTION).

▶ **Sopwith 1½ Strutter** two-seater N5624, in service with the RNAS at Mullion during the spring of 1917. The pilot and observer are both aboard. In the background is part of the huge windbreak shielding Mullion's main airship shed doors (JM BRUCE/GS LESLIE COLLECTION).

As well as airships, Mullion became a home for aircraft of the RNAS. In the spring of 1917, four Sopwith 1½ Strutter two-seat biplanes arrived to help with inshore submarine spotting along the southern Cornish coast, but left during August, desperately needed on the Western Front. However, 1½ Strutters returned to the Lizard in January 1918, while some low-powered de Havilland DH.6 training biplanes also turned up. In May and June, 515 and 516 (Special Duties) Flights respectively were formed from the DH.6s. 493 Flight was also created in May, equipped with larger, more reliable de Havilland DH.9s, but during August all three Flights became 236 Squadron. Six large canvas hangars were erected for Mullion's aircraft, between the north-western roadside fence and the larger of the huge airship sheds.

The U-boat war was also fought from other Cornish air bases, as the Channel network of aeroplane patrols grew. Gradually, a combined aerial deterrent was developed: floatplanes and landplanes employed on inshore patrols; airships, slow but with great endurance, and large flying-boats which provided a longer-range strike force. Royal Naval Air Station Newlyn (Land's End) was established in January 1917, built on a narrow apron near Newlyn's southern harbour wall. Newlyn operated bomb-carrying Short 184 and Fairey Hamble floatplanes. In March 1918 a base was commissioned at the hamlet of Crugmeer, near Padstow, as RNAS Padstow/Crugmeer. DH.6s began to arrive for inshore patrols.

Meanwhile, the Isles of Scilly saw the establishment of a flying-boat base on Tresco. Several sites among the islands were explored but felt too exposed to the variable climate, before a station was built at New Grimsby on the western side of Tresco, facing Bryher. RNAS Tresco was operational by February 1917, though with scanty facilities at first; one canvas hangar, some tents, a few wooden buildings. Six Curtiss H.12 twin-engined flying-boats were nominally on strength, but during February 1918 more substantial Felixstowe F.2A flying-boats began to arrive, followed by several F.3 'boats.

The DH.6s did not shine. Because they were underpowered, carrying bombs was a great chore; several aircraft sputtered into the seas off Cornwall following engine failures, though generally their sodden crews were picked up by passing boats. Newlyn's floatplanes had greater success. On 19 December 1917, Short 184 N1606 bombed and severely damaged a U-boat ten miles south-west of the Lizard. The submarine had been stalking a convoy of merchant ships and the aircrew noticed its torpedo track; following the Short's attack, oil and air bubbles were seen rising to the surface. Following this, on 24 March 1918 N1618 released two bombs at a U-boat and N1767 attacked a submarine on 6 May; N1616 claimed a suspected sinking on 16 May, while N2631 and N2958 made two separate attacks on 30 June. N1770 bombed an oil slick on 13 July, unsure of its cause but determined not to lose a possible opportunity; however, the result was unclear.

▲ Short 184 floatplane N1604, seen on its launching trolley at RNAS Newlyn during the summer of 1917. It is under power, and between the floats are mounted small bombs (J M Bruce/G S Leslie Collection).

▲ **A Royal Naval Air** Service Curtiss H.12 flying-boat, beached at the top of RNAS Tresco's slipway, New Grimsby, during 1917. The slipway is still there today (AUTHOR'S COLLECTION).

Aircraft from Tresco also engaged the U-boats. On 7 May 1917 the station's first submarine was claimed when H.12 flying-boat 8656 released two 100 lb bombs, both of which were reported to have struck, and the submarine submerged rapidly after its stern came high out of the water. The H.12 crew were awarded medals; many years later though, it was discovered the U-boat had survived and slunk away. On 10 May 1918, Tresco F.3 N4341 bombed and damaged the U-103. One of the last attacks of the war off Cornwall was made by a Tresco-based H.12B flying-boat on 11 October 1918, when it sighted a submarine wake four miles ahead of Convoy HH.71. Though the action was inconclusive, the U-boat retreated.

Finally, when the Armistice was signed on 11 November 1918, the terrible conflict ended. Anti-submarine patrols by Cornwall's airships and aircraft stopped once the U-boat commanders at sea had been told of the situation. During 1919 military aviation retreated from the Duchy as swiftly as it had arrived. Fittingly, Mullion's final airship flight was performed by the Mullion Twin, on 25 January. During February RNAS Newlyn was decommissioned and the airship outstation at Bude was vacated. Padstow/Crugmeer closed during March and Tresco in mid-May.

Inter War

Between the early nineteen-twenties and the mid-thirties a growth in 'air-mindedness' took place among Cornish people. During the immediate post-war years the sight of an aeroplane was still an exciting rarity, but trips to Cornwall by aerial joy-riding and barn-storming concerns gradually allowed thousands to become more familiar with aviation. Early in 1924, the Berkshire Aviation Company visited. They brought with them their redoubtable Avro 504K biplanes, flying from fields and putting on aerial shows across the Duchy, as well as offering short flights to bolder members of the public.

In Cornwall, a similar concern was created by Captain Percival Phillips, known in his local area of St Austell as PP. An ex-wartime flyer, Phillips established the Cornwall Aviation Company from his motor garage at Trewoon, just outside the town, ready for the 1924 summer season. He provided people with opportunities to experience short joy-rides, and witness stunt-flying the like of which will never be seen again.

Phillips' first aircraft was an Avro 504K biplane registered G-EBIZ, which he painted bright red. Though he flew many other Avros and different types over the years, G-EBIZ was PP's pride and joy; he gave it the affectionate pet-name Geebies. Over the next few summers, Phillips and his aeroplanes plied the Cornish resorts – Newquay, Fowey, Penzance and Perranporth were all visited – giving the public the chance to take short flights, no more than four minutes, using temporary landing-grounds rented from local farmers. As business grew, PP began to travel east beyond the Tamar. He would fly over each town where he was due to perform, dropping handbills to attract attention. Displays of stunt-flying and wing-walking also served as powerful advertising, while free flights

◀ **The Cornwall Aviation** Company operated from St Austell between 1924 and 1936. Here is the owner, Captain Percival Phillips, photographed with his first and favourite aircraft, Avro 504K G-EBIZ Geebies, near Newquay in around 1924 (AUTHOR'S COLLECTION).

▲ **A Cornwall Aviation** Company Avro, stunt-flying at Plymouth in the summer of 1932. The aircraft dives at the crowd as the wing-walker holds on by one hand to a single wire, in a display that by today's safety standards would be considered horrific (AUTHOR'S COLLECTION).

were offered to members of the local press in return for good publicity for the coming shows.

The charge for a passenger flight was five shillings, but for fifteen shillings the truly daring could experience a loop, or for one pound a spin. As the popularity of the flying displays grew, admittance was charged simply to enter the field and watch. Phillips' staff cheerfully performed aerial wing-walking stunts and would sometimes sit on the upper wings of the Avros, without any safety harnessing and held in place only by the pressure of the airflow. Each summer season during the late twenties and early thirties Phillips and his pilots ranged across Britain, followed by lorries containing the ground staff and aircraft spares, advertising hoardings, windsock and passenger ladders. And every autumn, the Avros returned to St Austell for overhaul, ready for next year's work.

But as time passed, the sight of a single Avro no longer held such fascination. The excitement of PP's shows began to pall as people became more familiar with the events, while occasional flying accidents caused bad publicity; during the 1930 season, poor weather added to the problems. PP teamed up with Sir Alan Cobham, the famous pilot and businessman, joining his National Aviation Days Display flying circus for its 1932 British tour, and the following season joined forces with the British Hospitals Air Pageant, visiting Bodmin, Truro and

Falmouth during a very busy summer itinerary all across Britain. But at the end of the 1936 season Percival Phillips finally shut the books on the Cornwall Aviation Company, though he continued with other aviation interests.

\ʕ↺ʔ/

By the mid nineteen-thirties passenger air transport had blossomed in Britain, cities linked by new and developing airlines. In Cornwall, commercial flying began with the small company of Provincial Airways Ltd. From April 1934, Provincial flew a summer season link between Plymouth and Hayle, two flights per day in each direction. The company used a de Havilland DH.84 Dragon biplane which carried six passengers; the journey took forty-five minutes. By August, Provincial's services included another Cornish stop at Trebelzue Big Field, overlooking Watergate Bay near Newquay. The following summer Trebelzue was used again, while the westernmost terminus became a field outside Penzance. Unfortunately though, like many of its contemporaries Provincial went into liquidation, and the service ended in September 1935.

▲ **During the summers** of 1933 and 1934 Sir Alan Cobham's National Aviation Days Display flying circus visited Padstow, bringing its tri-motor Airspeed Ferry passenger biplane. Here in front of the aircraft we see (L-R) Nick Reynolds, Sam Phillips and his son Charles, Harry Champion, Sgt Trays, Mr Lane, Mr Ford-Hutchinson, Robert Warne, and Peter Ford-Hutchinson (MALCOLM MCCARTHY COLLECTION).

◄ **Channel Air Ferries** de Havilland DH.84 Dragon G-ACPY, on the Land's End – Isles of Scilly service during the late 1930s. By the wooden steps up to the cabin a lady passenger stands in the slipstream of the engine, her hat jammed firmly on her head (AUTHOR'S COLLECTION).

Meanwhile, in addition to his flying circus activities Alan Cobham had started an airline of his own, Cobham Air Routes Ltd. Cobham considered establishing a link between Penzance and the Isles of Scilly, and secured landing rights for a commercial service. Subsequently though he sold his airline, and the rights, to aviator and rival airline owner Captain Gordon Olley, who registered a new service as Channel Air Ferries on 8 May 1936. Olley then set about finding a suitable landing ground for his new westernmost route.

The location he chose for the Penzance aerodrome was between Little Kelynack and Brea Downs, a short distance from St Just though the site quickly became known as Land's End. It consisted simply of a landing field, one hangar, a tiny wooden booking office, a fuel store and basic servicing equipment. The Isles of Scilly's airfield was even smaller, located at the north-western part of St Mary's and, because suitable space was at such a premium, placed partly on the golf-course.

Channel's first scheduled flight left Land's End on 15 September 1937, using DH.84 Dragon biplane G-ADCR piloted by Captain D L Dustin, a New Zealander. Four passengers were carried, departing at 9.00 am and arriving at St Mary's twenty minutes later. Five people made the return trip, touching down at Land's End at 10.10 am. The airfare was £1.0.0 for a single ticket, £1.15.0 (£1.75) return, and to begin with, just one flight a day was made in each direction. Tickets were interchangeable with those for the Isles of Scilly Steamship Company, and a motor-bus service linked the airfield with Penzance. As its popularity grew, during the following April the service was increased to thrice daily at the weekends, and in May an additional Sunday evening service was made available by request. A small DH.83 Fox Moth biplane arrived at Land's End to provide pleasure flights. In May too, Channel began a service from Land's End to Plymouth, and on to Bristol.

But by the end of 1938, a rationalisation of several British air lines had taken place. As part of that process, Channel Air Ferries was absorbed by Great Western and Southern Air Lines. The new company continued the service between Land's End and St Mary's, and the fleet of de Havilland passenger biplanes grew. Over the summer of 1939, each day up to eight return trips were flown.

Toward the end of the thirties too, further airfields appeared in Cornwall. During 1937 a site was established at St Merryn, near Padstow, by a company named St Merryn Aerodrome Ltd. William Rhodes-Moorhouse, son of the famous First World War airman, who lived at Constantine Bay, assisted with the new venture. Refuelling facilities were installed and the strip was billed as Cornwall's first public airfield, though in fact it was little used. At Treligga, north-west of Delabole, a field was adopted as a gliding site by the newly-formed Cornwall Gliding Club. Gliding enthusiasts also flew at Summercourt, at first using a catapult to launch their gliders but later a car tow. Practice gliding took place on the slopes of Rosenannon Downs, St Wenn, while a further group flew occasionally from the beach at Marazion.

Commercial passenger services also expanded during the late thirties. Western Airways had been started back in 1932 based at Weston-super-Mare, and had grown steadily. During May 1939, Western began a service from Swansea to Penzance via Barnstaple and Newquay, leaving Wales at 12.00 noon and terminating at 1.45 pm. The return journeys commenced at 2.25 pm, arriving back at Swansea at 4.10 pm. At Newquay, Western flew from Trebelzue Big Field, which by then had become an official AA Landing Ground. Trebelzue Farm, adjoining the airfield, began to offer food and accommodation for passengers.

▲ **Western Airways' Dragon** G-ACMJ was frequently used on that company's Cornish services, operating from landing strips at Ludgvan and Trebelzue (NEVILLE DOYLE).

▲ **Occasionally, waterborne military** aircraft visited Falmouth's harbour on exercises. Here, a Saunders-Roe London II flying-boat of 201 Squadron is moored off Trefusis Point, during the summer of 1939 (AUTHOR'S COLLECTION).

Near Penzance, a small airfield was opened outside Ludgvan to serve the town. Western Airways also used Dragons on its Cornish route; its services ran until September 1939.

Over the summer of 1939, facilities at St Mary's were improved after Great Western and Southern Air Lines agreed a lease for a new landing ground; the golf-course arrangement was no longer suitable for the volume of traffic. An area at High Cross, overlooking Old Town, was set aside as a proper airfield, being used for the first time on 25 July and officially opened on 16 August. By September the Land's End – St Mary's route had carried some 10,000 passengers, 18,000 lb of freight and 5,000 lb of newspapers since its beginnings in September 1937. During that period, the advertising slogan was the unwittingly ambiguous 'twenty minutes and you're over'!

But as the nineteen-thirties progressed, gradually the threat emerged of another conflict with Germany. Rearmament of Britain's forces began, slowly at first but with increasing urgency. During 1937 the first surveys of possible sites for military airfields in Cornwall were carried out by the RAF. As international events accelerated, the compulsory purchase of land for military uses, including the construction of new airfields, was introduced under the Emergency Powers (Defence) Act of 1939. Once more the strategically important location of Cornwall saw to it that the Duchy was involved in the buildup. By September 1939, plans were well in hand to utilise Cornwall's position and resources for the coming war.

The Second World War

Immediately following the declaration of war, on 3 September 1939 British commercial aviation was drastically cut by legislation which forbade all civilian flights over the east of England and Scotland. For each such flight in any other area, special licences were required. The Land's End – St Mary's link was one of the few services allowed to continue. Great Western and Southern's Dragons were quickly camouflaged, their cabin windows painted over to prevent passengers taking photographs of shipping, landing lights masked out. Service departure times were varied to avoid routine noticeable to the Germans.

By then the first new Cornish military airfield was open for business, though generally its work was undramatic. This was RAF Cleave, four miles north of Bude on the cliff-top near the village of Kilkhampton. The station was used for anti-aircraft gunnery training, and had received its first aircraft when No 1 Anti-Aircraft Co-operation Unit had begun to arrive in May 1939, flying elderly target-towing Westland Wallace biplanes and pilotless radio-controlled Queen Bee target drones.

Autumn saw the opening of RAF St Eval, around five miles north-east of Newquay. Planning of the new airfield had begun two years previously after it

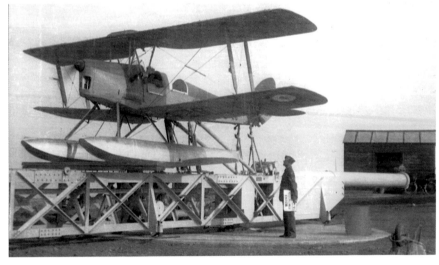

▲ A De Havilland Queen Bee pilotless target floatplane of V Flight, No. 1 Anti Aircraft Co-operation Unit, being prepared for launch over the sea from the catapult at RAF Cleave during 1940 (BILL YOUNG via TIM BISHOP).

had been concluded that once again, aerial patrols off Cornwall might be necessary. St Eval was designed to accommodate two general reconnaissance squadrons. Twin-engined Avro Ansons of 217 Squadron arrived in October for convoy protection and anti-submarine work over the Channel and the Irish Sea, long arduous duties in the same spirit as their First World War forebears.

In December 1939 the Admiralty requisitioned 550 acres of land for a new Naval Air Station near St Merryn, to be used for training. Construction began in the new year of 1940. Four runways were laid, one of which swallowed up the area used earlier by St Merryn Aerodrome Ltd. During March the Admiralty acquired further land, at the pre-war Treligga gliding site, for use as an air-to-ground firing range.

Meanwhile, at St Eval 217 Squadron's Ansons were supplemented by detachments of Armstrong Whitworth Whitleys from 58 Squadron Bomber Command, more substantial aircraft able to carry a greater bomb load. Later, Bristol Beaufort bombers and torpedo-bombers also arrived. On 2 April 1940 the first attack by a St Eval-based aircraft on a U-boat was made when Anson 'P'

Battle of Britain: Cornwall's RAF Organisation

By the summer of 1940, with France fallen and the Battle of Britain raging, Cornwall entered the frontline of the air war over the United Kingdom. At St Eval, in addition to the Coastal Command presence which had existed since the beginning of the war, aircraft from Fighter Command arrived.

Cornwall's fighters came under the command of No. 10 Group RAF with its headquarters at Rudloe Manor, Wiltshire, headed by Air Vice-Marshal Sir Christopher Quintin Brand. By August 1940, at St Eval the Group controlled 234 Squadron (Spitfires) and later 230 Squadron (Hurricanes). As well as this, from time to time detachments of 247 Squadron's Gloster Gladiator biplane fighters, and later its Hurricanes, were flown to St Eval from

Roborough airfield in Devon, to provide additional cover.

Meanwhile, No. 15 (General Reconnaissance) Group, commanded by Air Commodore R G Parry, was responsible for RAF Coastal Command's operations over western England and the Irish Sea. At St Eval, by the summer of 1940 217 Squadron was in the process of converting from its elderly Avro Ansons to more modern Bristol Beauforts for bombing, sea-mining and anti-submarine patrols, though that wasn't completed until December. That summer too, an additional force arrived at the station in the shape of 236 Squadron, which brought Bristol Blenheim fighters for overwater reconnaissance duties.

of 217 Squadron released two bombs; a patch of oil appeared on the water, but that evidence was not sufficient to claim a kill.

In June 1940 France fell, and Cornwall became vulnerable to the attentions of the Luftwaffe; on 18 June, Spitfires of 234 Squadron arrived at St Eval for defensive duties. The Duchy was bombed for the first time on 5 July. During that month 234 Squadron destroyed three German Junkers Ju 88 bombers, one 25 miles south-east of Land's End on the 8th, another in the same spot on the 27th and the third some 35 miles south-east of Plymouth on the 28th during a daylight raid. Over the summer and autumn of 1940 St Eval was attacked several times, with loss of life and several aircraft destroyed; Cleave was also bombed.

On 10 August St Merryn airfield was commissioned as HMS Vulture, receiving its first naval training units. These were 774 Squadron, an armament training unit operating Blackburn Rocs and Skuas, as well as Fairey Swordfish biplanes; and 792 Squadron which also employed Rocs and Skuas (later replaced by Defiants and Martinets) as an air target-towing unit. Both were long-term residents; 774 Squadron stayed until October 1944, 792 until it was disbanded in January 1945. St Merryn's building programme had lagged, so billets for its personnel were acquired in the village as well as at the Yellowsands Hotel at Harlyn Bay and Woodlands, a country house at Treator, near Padstow. During October and November 1940 the station was bombed, but managed to continue its training work.

The spring of 1941 marked a big step forward in Cornwall's fighter operations; between March and May, three new airfields opened. The site chosen for Cornwall's main fighter base was Nancekuke Common, near Portreath on the north coast. It was decided the new station would be supported by two further airfields, one at Perranporth hosting day-fighters, the other at Predannack for night-fighters. RAF Portreath opened on 7 March 1941 as a new Fighter Command Sector Headquarters. Its first occupants were 263 Squadron's Whirlwind twin-engined fighters, replaced by the Spitfires of 152 Squadron and Hurricanes of 247 Squadron which arrived during April and early May respectively. In fact though, demarcation between day and night-fighter duties became blurred. Over their lives the three stations hosted a wide variety of Squadrons and operations, particularly Portreath which became deeply committed to aircraft ferrying activities.

During early April, photographs taken over Brest of the German battlecruiser Gneisenau revealed it had left dry dock. Plans were at once made for an attack; St Eval's Beauforts were given the job. Unfortunately, before the mission two aircraft sank in muddy ground at the airfield, and two further Beauforts became lost in cloud during the flight out on 6 April. However, Scotsman F/O Kenneth

Radar in Cornwall

Though September 1939 found Britain ill-prepared in many ways for war, one tremendous asset was an operational radar system capable of detecting incoming enemy aircraft. Initially, an array of twenty radar stations was positioned along Britain's vulnerable south-east coast, known as Chain Home. The radar controllers became adept at liaising with RAF operations rooms, which in turn directed fighter aircraft to intercept the German raiders. During the early part of the war the radar stations were added to, as Chain Home coverage was extended along the southwest shoreline. Further developments in technology led to the introduction of the Chain Home Low radar, capable of detecting enemy aircraft closer to the ground than previously, as well as shipping movements.

By April 1941, Cornwall was host to seven Chain Home and Chain Home Low radar stations, and the network grew steadily. Eventually, Chain Home stations were constructed at Downderry, Torpoint; Dry Tree, Goonhilly; Sennen, West Penwith; Trelanvean, Goonhilly; and Trerew, Newquay. Stations equipped with Chain Home Low radars appeared at Chapel Carn Brea, Carnanton; Dry Tree, Goonhilly; Dunderhole Point, near Tintagel; Jacka Point, Portloe; Mark's Castle, Penwith; Pen Olver, on The Lizard; Rame Head; Trevose Head; and Trewavas Head in Mount's Bay.

After the war, Cornwall's military radar stations were decommissioned. Today, though, much evidence survives of their existence. For those who wish to explore, some of the old bases are hard to find – good hunting!

Campbell, flying N1016, pressed home his attack and made his run into the target at around thirty feet; he would have been looking up at the superstructure of the German vessel. Campbell released his torpedo at point-blank range and scored a direct hit on the Gneisenau, damaging her severely below the waterline. The Beaufort, though, was hit by intense anti-aircraft fire and crashed into the harbour. Campbell was posthumously awarded the Victoria Cross; he was 23 years old.

RAF Perranporth opened on 28 April 1941, perched high on the cliff-top between St Agnes and Perranporth. Spitfires of 66 Squadron arrived from Exeter for the defence of coastal towns and coverage of the south-west sea lanes. Over the course of the summer the airfield's hangars, earthworks and two further runways were completed.

In May 1941 RAF Predannack came into being, south of Mullion village on the Lizard, a short cycle away from the old First World War RNAS airship site.

Because of the pressing need for fighter cover against air-raids, Predannack too was occupied while still incomplete; 247 Squadron and their Hurricanes arrived from Portreath in mid-June. A detachment of all-black night-fighter Beaufighters from 600 Squadron also appeared. 247 Squadron's first success came on 7 July when a Junkers Ju 88 bomber was destroyed off Falmouth, diving into the sea ablaze. Over the summer of 1941, Portreath, Perranporth and Predannack all built up strength and their civil works were rounded off.

In the same month as Predannack opened, a westernmost fighter outpost was formed when the Isles of Scilly received Hurricanes. On 19 May six aircraft from 87 Squadron squeezed onto the small grass strip on St Mary's, led by Squadron Leader Ian Gleed DFC, on what the squadron records described as a 'fishing expedition'. Within hours of 87's arrival, an alert was raised and two aircraft took off in search of the intruder, one piloted by Pilot Officer I J Badger, the other by Gleed. Some five miles out, Badger found an Arado 196 floatplane which he sent into the sea. The Squadron's second victory from St Mary's came on 24 May, when a Dornier Do 18 flying-boat was shot down by Gleed and his wingman.

At Land's End, civil flights to and from St Mary's had been much reduced, but the service continued almost uninterrupted until 3 June 1941, when Dragon G-ACPY disappeared. A search was made by aircraft and by the Scilly lifeboat Cunard but of the pilot and five passengers, only one body was found. For some time it was thought the Dragon had fallen victim to a prowling Ju 88. However,

▲ **Summer 1941**: an RAF Predannack-based Hurricane of 247 Squadron sits among the station's building detritus prior to a mission (ANDREW THOMAS).

it was later established the aggressor had been a Heinkel He 111 bomber returning to Nantes from an aborted attack on the Barrow-in-Furnace shipyards. The Heinkel had used Scilly as a navigation point and had chanced on the defenceless aircraft, which it machine-gunned. The Dragon, its port engine in flames, had crashed into the sea. A replacement arrived, the service continued.

During 1941, first steps were made to take the fight to the enemy across the Channel, when detachments of Blenheim light bombers began flying from Cornwall to raid the French coast. From July they were given Spitfire escort by 130 (Punjab) Squadron based at Portreath. Several other fighter squadrons from the Portreath sector also provided escorts, including 152, 66 and 234 Squadrons. 313 (Czech) Squadron arrived there during August, their Spitfires carrying out intruder sweeps over northern France. During August Predannack's Hurricanes also began missions into France. By then, the Portreath fighter operations room was sometimes in charge of as many as seven squadrons, from Perranporth and Predannack as well as Portreath itself, often as cover for the raiding Blenheims.

In September 1941, the new Coastal Command airfield RAF Trebelzue opened. The pre-war Big Field had been requisitioned as a satellite for St Eval, originally with thoughts of use as an Emergency Landing Ground. For a time Trebelzue also acted as a nocturnal retreat for St Eval's aircraft, to avoid their destruction during the air raids there.

৩৵২

During February 1942, St Eval was notified that the German battlecruisers Scharnhorst and Gneisenau were about to leave the haven of Brest harbour. Immediately another attack was planned; 22 Squadron's Beaufort bombers prepared to make a strike on the night of 11/12 February. Eight bomb-carrying Hurricanes of 402 (Royal Canadian Air Force) Squadron arrived at Perranporth to add to the firepower, their targets five destroyers which it was believed would escort the larger ships out of Brest. Radar-carrying Hudson aircraft would assist with the attack.

However, bad luck dogged the operation. The weather was poor, while one of the patrolling Hudsons developed a fault with its radar and had to return home. A marauding Ju 88 caused one of the remaining Hudsons to switch off its radar during evasive manoeuvres, while another happened to be scanning in the wrong direction during the critical time. This unfortunate combination allowed the enemy ships to slip away unchallenged. As a consolation prize, during their return journey to Brest the Hurribombers found and attacked the destroyers off the coast of Brittany, sinking one and damaging another.

▲ **Spitfire VBs of** 130 Squadron line up on the clifftop at RAF Perranporth in readiness for a patrol during early 1942 (DENYS BRYANT).

Spring 1942 saw the arrival at St Eval of 53 Squadron (Hudsons), the balance of 58 Squadron (Whitleys) and 502 Squadron (also Whitleys) to improve efforts in the U-boat war. By then, the Hurricanes on St Mary's had become known as 1449 Flight, with six pilots and thirty-one ground-crew. Much of the unit's activities involved escort of damaged Allied bombers returning from the Continent.

Meanwhile, Trebelzue's future has come under scrutiny. The need had grown for another airfield dedicated to ferrying, at a rate estimated at a hundred aircraft each month, but Trebelzue was felt too small for the task. The RAF decided to start again by building a new, larger station a little to the east with three runways of adequate length, while keeping Trebelzue as a dispersal area; construction began during mid-August.

In April 1942 St Merryn became home to 762 Squadron, operating Fulmars, Masters and Martlets as an Advanced Flying Training School squadron. The base also hosted a number of Squadrons for air-to-air and air-to-ground gunnery practice. Typical were 804 and 880 Squadrons, who stayed for a month or so with their Sea Hurricanes.

By the summer, Cleave's Anti-Aircraft Co-operation Units had shed their aged Wallace biplanes and were flying newer Hawker Henley monoplane target-tugs, generally for the benefit of the anti-aircraft practice ranges at Penhale and Cameron Camp, St Agnes, as well as Cleave's own. Numerous Queen Bee target

Overseas Aircraft Dispatch Unit

The Overseas Aircraft Dispatch Unit (OADU) was formed at RAF Honeybourne, Worcestershire, in October 1941, its remit to co-ordinate ferry flight of military aircraft to far-flung theatres of operations. A detachment of the unit (1 OADU) was established at RAF Portreath. The Cornish station became used as the starting-point for long-range journeys made by squadrons and aircraft posted to North Africa and the Middle East. The first customers ferried through Portreath were four B-17C Fortress heavy bombers en route for Egypt. Often Portreath grew congested as travelling aircraft and crews awaited their departure, particularly if the weather was poor and a backlog accumulated; rows of bell tents were erected to provide overflow accommodation. As well as the B-17s, a wide variety of other aircraft passed through: Blenheims, Beaufighters, Wellingtons, an Ensign, an Albatross, even the sole Cunliffe-Owen OA-1 'wide-body', on its way for use by Free French forces in North Africa.

When the weather was bad, sometimes over a hundred aircraft would collect on the airfield at once. Despite the density of traffic, generally accidents were light, but 8 December 1942 was a black day at Portreath; first a Lockheed Hudson, then a Bristol Beaufort flew into nearby cliffs after take-off. The first half of the following year saw the station almost entirely committed to ferry movements. A total of 237 aircraft were dispatched during January 1943, 283 in February and 317 in March, a truly formidable rate way over the original estimates.

Ferrying operations continued until the end of the war, and in May 1945 the OADU was transferred to 44 Group (Ferry Service), Transport Command; over that month, two hundred aircraft were delivered overseas. During September though, with a sharp decline in ferrying requirements, Portreath's remaining tasks were taken over by St Mawgan, where 2 OADU had been established for similar work. St Mawgan also dealt with American and Canadian aircraft returning home from Britain and Europe, and acted as an assembly point for aircraft destined for the rebuilding French Air Force. By the autumn of 1945, no fewer than twenty-eight thousand aircraft movements had been carried out by the station from the time it had opened for business. As well as the variable weather, so many 'strangers' passing through Cornish airspace in the form of ferried aircraft must have made activities very tricky on some occasions.

aircraft remained; considering their role, several achieved remarkable longevity.

During July, St Eval received the Whitleys of 10 Operational Training Unit, to further ease the burden of the interminable U-boat patrols. Naturally though, the unit's trainee crews were inexperienced and three aircraft were lost in that month alone; two went missing over the Bay of Biscay, while a third crashed on the station boundary. However, on 17 July a U-boat was destroyed by a combination of a St Eval Whitley and a Lancaster. Following that success, on 16 August a B-24 Liberator heavy bomber of 120 Squadron from Predannack attacked and damaged the U-89 with depth charges. That strike marked the beginning of Squadron Leader Terry Bulloch's career in anti-submarine operations; he became the RAF's most successful U-boat hunter. Two days later, Bulloch and his Liberator attacked and severely damaged the U-653; both submarines were forced to put in to Brest for repairs.

On 19 August 1942 Operation Jubilee took place, and Portreath contributed to the air cover for the ill-fated Dieppe landings. Eight days later, the people of Penzance had a surprise when a 51 Squadron Whitley passed low over the town following engine failure, and put down on Eastern Green beach. Its crew could truly count their blessings for not only did they all survive, but quite by chance the aircraft managed to avoid the beach's mined areas.

Over that summer, detachments of Mosquito twin-engined fighter-bombers arrived at Predannack; 410 (RCAF) Squadron for escort work, and 25 Squadron for patrols over Biscay. 11 June saw an encounter between three 25 Squadron aircraft, plus three of 456 Squadron, and five Ju 88s, some 130 miles off the northern tip of Spain. In the exchange, Flt Lt Joe Singleton of 25 Squadron destroyed one enemy aircraft, which dived into the sea following the loss of its port engine. Two more Ju 88s were damaged. However, on 13 June 25 Squadron lost three Mosquitoes, all shot down over Biscay.

On 1 October a new Cornish airfield became operational, taken on charge by 19 Group, Coastal Command as part of the anti U-boat campaign. This was RAF Davidstow Moor, situated two miles north-east of Camelford near the northern part of Bodmin Moor, the highest operational airfield in the United Kingdom at 970 feet above sea level. In fact its use by 19 Group was delayed at first, because of an American presence there in support of Operation Torch, the allied invasion of North Africa. Eighth Air Force Fortress and Liberator bombers were the main occupants, using Davidstow as a staging-post between their bases in East Anglia and their European targets, which included St Nazaire's U-boat pens.

On 24 February 1943, Trebelzue airfield was renamed RAF St Mawgan. By then, new runways were being built east of the old site, longer, wider, of better quality and more favourably oriented. At Perranporth, facilities were increased to reflect the frequent presence of three fighter squadrons there, and the runways were lengthened. 412 (RCAF) Falcon Squadron brought its Spitfires in April, accompanied by 610 Squadron also with Spitfires; both began coastal patrols and sweeps over France.

During March, detachments from the Mosquitos of 456 Squadron and 307 Lvov Squadron moved to Predannack, the first Poles to serve at the station. April saw the arrival of Predannack's first full Mosquito Squadron, 264, used for reconnaissance and maritime attack over the Channel and Biscay. By then, the station's strength had grown to well over 1,500 personnel.

On 1 May 1943 no fewer than fifteen American Eighth Air Force B-17 Fortress bombers landed at Predannack, having met fierce German fighter opposition on a raid over St Nazaire. Fortress 42-29649 of 306th Bomb Group staggered in, badly damaged; its ball turret gunner, Staff Sergeant Maynard H Smith, on his first mission, had fought a series of fierce fires amid exploding

▲ **Fairey Swordfish target** tug P4086 S6-D of 774 Squadron, the armament training unit for telegraphist air gunners and observers, surrounded by industrious naval cadet helpers at St Merryn during the summer of 1943 (AUTHOR'S COLLECTION).

▲ Davidstow-based Wellington XIV of 304 (Slaski) Squadron, flown by Polish personnel, September 1943. In the background, another Wellington and the hump of Bray Down, situated south-west of the airfield (ROD KNIGHT).

ammunition for over ninety minutes, made the injured rear gunner comfortable, and jettisoned all he could from the failing aircraft. The fires had severely weakened 42-29649, but the Fortress held together until it landed, skidding to a halt in two charred sections. S/Sgt Smith later received the first Medal of Honor awarded to a living member of the Eighth Air Force.

At St Merryn the opening months of 1943 saw yet more construction work, to prepare for the appearance of the School of Air Combat and their Seafires. By the early summer the RAF was making a play for St Merryn, seeking to use it for the maintenance of St Eval's aircraft and offering Talbenny in south-west Wales in exchange. However, the Navy managed to hold on to its Cornish station.

St Mawgan was completed over the summer of 1943. In May, Whitley glider-tugs of 297 Squadron were exercised there, towing Horsa gliders, in preparation for the Allied invasion of Sicily known as Operation Husky. During June the 491st Base and Air Base Squadron of the American Air Transport Command appeared with their Liberators. The first of the new runways was opened on 1 July, and another American caller dropped in: tastefully-named Liberator Big Dick. By August, the old Trebelzue airfield had been reduced to a dispersal area.

By the summer too, 19 Group RAF had recovered Davidstow airfield from the Americans. Daylight anti-submarine work by 304 Slaski (Polish) Squadron and 547 Squadron began over Biscay, both units flying Wellington bombers.

The work was dangerous; the U-boats had taken to sailing in packs and instead of submerging at the sight of an aircraft would sometimes fight it out on the surface, where they could put up stiff defensive fire using their deck guns.

During October, four Wellingtons and a single Halifax of 192 Squadron arrived at Davidstow. The role of 192 Squadron was highly-classified, a radar countermeasures function involving the identification of enemy radar types, patterns and wavelengths. The aircraft made numerous flights over Biscay, working against the German radar which monitored Coastal Command's anti-submarine patrols. The detachment continued its clandestine work until the following summer.

FIDO

Cornish weather can change rapidly and become most inhospitable; thick, clinging fog is sometimes experienced, particularly over the moorland areas. In the early war years, on numerous occasions aircrew based in Cornwall returned home from a mission only to find it impossible to set down, their airfields fogbound, leading to forced landings with empty fuel tanks.

The government's Petroleum Warfare Department, established in July 1940, was tasked with developing a means of overcoming fogbound airfields. The result was FIDO, or Fog Investigation and Dispersal Operation. Alongside airfield runways, lines of burners were installed, fuelled by petrol, to burn off nearby fog and allow safe flying operations. Early experiments and development of the system were daunting, at times terrifying, usage of precious imported fuel extravagant. But though it was not always completely effective, FIDO saved lives.

Eventually, the system was installed countrywide across fifteen British airfields.

In Cornwall, FIDO featured at two airfields. RAF Davidstow Moor, nearly a thousand feet above sea level, prone to extremes of weather, was the first European airfield to trial FIDO, in August 1943. The system was a portable one, and was first used successfully by a pilot who landed en route to St Merryn in a Tiger Moth. After a month, the system was transported to RAF St Eval. Through the following winter a more permanent FIDO was installed at St Eval, its first operational usage in April 1944 when a 304 Squadron maritime patrol Wellington landed safely there. The system continued in service until the end of the war, its final recorded use during May 1945 when three Wellingtons landed successfully; a fourth was diverted elsewhere. The fuel bill? One hundred and twenty thousand gallons!

Up to the autumn of 1943 Perranporth had operated wholly Spitfires, but in September 183 Squadron brought their bomb-carrying Typhoons, to attack enemy shipping and airfields. However, the new arrivals found the runways uncomfortably short and in October they transferred south to Predannack. The following month, rocket-armed Swordfish biplanes also moved to Predannack, used for air-to-ground rocket trials at Loe Pool on the Lizard.

$\wp\wr\wp$

The first half of 1944 saw a huge military buildup across southern England in support of the coming Allied invasion of northern France. Operations from Cornwall continued relentlessly. From early that year, St Eval hosted three Liberator bomber squadrons on anti-submarine work; 224, 53, and 547; on 3 January, 224 Squadron aircraft severely damaged the U-373. In mid-February the Mosquitos of 248 Squadron arrived at Portreath for strike operations over the Channel and Biscay; transfer of some of Portreath's transport work across to St Mawgan allowed a greater offensive role for the old fighter station. A fierce battle

▲ A Beaufighter of 404 (Royal Canadian Air Force) Squadron, under power at RAF Davidstow Moor during the summer of 1944. The ground crew are priming its rail-mounted rockets prior to an anti-shipping mission (ROYAL CANADIAN AIR FORCE).

took place on 10 March, when six Mosquitos flying off northern Spain found several German vessels sailing under a protective umbrella of ten Junkers Ju 88s. Two German aircraft were destroyed and the convoy attacked, without loss. On 25 March two 248 Squadron Mosquitos attacked and destroyed the U-976 off the Ile de Yeu, while two days later the same aircraft damaged the U-960.

During the spring, Davidstow too became a centre of increased offensive activities. In April, 524 Squadron arrived with Wellingtons for anti-E-boat patrols. During the following month the Beaufighters of 144 and 404 (RCAF) Squadrons were posted there, also for anti-shipping duties, being christened 154 (GR) Wing. On 6 May, the secretive 192 Squadron made its last Special Duties flight from Davidstow.

235 Squadron (Beaufighters) moved to Portreath in April, joining 248 Squadron to form 153 (GR) Wing as the buildup to D-Day continued. On 11 April Portreath's Mosquitos and Beaufighters were involved in a savage exchange when they attacked a disabled U-boat covered by twelve Ju 88s, four of which were destroyed and five damaged. A Mosquito and two Beaufighters were also lost, the U-boat left sinking. Guarded by Mosquitos, Air Sea Rescue aircraft arrived at the scene to check for survivors of the encounter. More Ju 88s appeared; three were shot down for the loss of a single Mosquito. During their stay at Portreath, 235 Squadron converted from Beaufighters to Mosquitos.

On 11 April too, Predannack's 151 Squadron met with success. During an anti-shipping strike off St Nazaire, twelve Ju 88s were spied at wave-top height, shepherding a surfaced U-boat and several flak ships. 151's Mosquitos destroyed three Ju 88s and damaged two others while a flak ship was also hit. Later that day a second engagement took place, when three more enemy aircraft were shot down; however, two Mosquitos were also lost. On 4 May, 151 Squadron's Wg Cdr G H Goodman found three Heinkel He 111 bombers just west of Dijon which unusually, he attacked from below, destroying them all. Shortly afterwards he sighted a fourth He 111, which he also dispatched.

On 6 June, D-Day, the movement was reported of three German destroyers and escorting aircraft, from the Geronde estuary on a heading for Brest and in the direction of the Allied invasion fleet. That evening, thirty-one rocket-armed Beaufighters of 154 Wing left Davidstow and joined up with ten 248 Squadron Mosquitos over Land's End. In the ensuing strike off Belle-Île, two of the destroyers were damaged and an accompanying Ju 188 was shot down; just prior to midnight a second attack was mounted. Two days later, one of the damaged destroyers, by that time beached, was strafed and wrecked by the Beaufighters, with an escort of Spitfires provided by Predannack.

▲ **RAF St Eval**, summer 1944. A Coastal Command Liberator receives its complement of depth charges before setting off on an anti-submarine patrol (AUTHOR'S COLLECTION).

Two days following D-Day, a 224 Squadron Liberator flying from St Eval piloted by Canadian Flt Lt Kenneth Moore despatched two U-boats, the U-629 and the U-373, within half an hour in separate low-level attacks between the Isles of Scilly and Ushant. Flt Lt Moore received the DSO for those actions. The U-821 was destroyed a few miles off Ushant on 10 June, by a combination of four 248 Squadron Mosquitos and a 206 Squadron Liberator. On 12 June, a 224 Squadron Liberator damaged the U-441 but itself failed to return, while two weeks later a Liberator from 311 Squadron sank the U-971 using a combination of rockets and depth-charges. Finally that frantic month, on 29 June Liberator L of 224 Squadron sank the U-998.

For the whole of June following D-Day the Predannack-based Spitfires, usually armed with two 500 lb bombs, attacked German shipping and coastal radar installations. Frequently too they ranged inland, striking at airfields, goods trains and German road traffic. Often, Predannack's Spitfire Wing flew from dawn to dusk.

The Beaufighters of 404 and 236 Squadrons continued their anti-shipping strikes from Davidstow until August. On 8 August, fifteen 404 and nine 236 aircraft combined in a sweep south of Lorient and found four enemy minesweepers, all of which they set afire, though one aircraft was lost. Four days later the 7,000 ton vessel Sauerland was attacked off La Pallice and left burning. On 20 August twenty Beaufighters mauled a flak ship, a minesweeper and two destroyers in the Bay though the return fire was fierce and many of the aircraft were damaged; three force-landed in France and one ditched, though its crew survived.

But following the feverish rate of operations over the summer, as the war in Europe moved eastward the pace of Cornwall's aviation activity began to ease off. At the end of August Davidstow's Beaufighters left, and on 19 September the airfield ceased to be operational. St Mary's saw 1449 Flight disbanded, also in September, and the airfield was reduced to Care and Maintenance standing. By VE Day, Predannack had no Squadrons at all, while Cleave and Perranporth assumed Care and Maintenance status during May 1945.

The Mosquitos of 151 and 406 Squadrons returned to Predannack during May, though with the sudden end of the war in the Far East 406 disbanded. Predannack soldiered on until June when it too was reduced to Care and Maintenance. However, the airfield experienced a brief resurgence during the autumn; on 15 September a great air display took place to mark Battle of Britain Day. Over four thousand people travelled to the Lizard to watch the flying and admire the static aircraft. The participating types included Spitfires, Harvards, Tempests, Mustangs, Vengeances, Mosquitos, Warwicks and Lancasters, while a flypast was performed at the end of the day by nine Mosquitos of 151 Squadron. The display was Predannack's last important event before the station finally closed; gently, nature began to reclaim the abandoned runways.

Portreath's air traffic control facilities closed in October and the station was placed under the control of St Eval as non-active. In November Cleave closed while during December, Care and Maintenance status followed for Portreath, and Davidstow finally shut down. Perranporth transferred to 44 Group, Transport Command in February 1946, but there were no further aircraft movements and closure came during April.

St Eval continued, as did St Mawgan for a time. St Merryn's post-war future too looked reasonably rosy; during August 1945, 725 Squadron arrived with its Martinet target tugs, becoming an Air Target Towing Unit. In the same month 748 Squadron, formed at St Merryn as a Fighter Pool squadron during the dark days of October 1942, returned with Wildcats, Seafires and a few Corsairs, as 10 Naval Operational Training Unit.

Post War

In the new post-war world, thoughts turned to the resuscitation of civil air travel. Great Western and Southern Air Lines' route between Land's End and St Mary's had been one of the few that had stayed open during almost the entire course of the war. The service continued, but under new ownership; British European Airways took over nearly all internal scheduled air routes inside the United Kingdom. Great Western was acquired on 1 February 1947.

A scattering of concerns evaded BEA. The independent charter company Island Air Services flew two Proctor light aircraft from St Mary's until the autumn of 1948, for pleasure flips and transport of flowers to the mainland. Another short-lived commercial operation began the following summer, when Aquila Airways commenced charter flights carrying holidaymakers between Falmouth and St Mary's, using civilianised Sunderland flying-boats. During the early 1950s, Fingland Aviation brought tourists down from Manchester using Avro Ansons, while the Proctors of Murray Chown Aviation connected Staverton and Cardiff with Cornwall.

But it was BEA's Land's End – St Mary's service which proved by far the most popular and enduring Cornish route. By the late forties, flights were in full-swing and during the 1953 season over 36,000 people were carried. The Dragons had been replaced by Dragon Rapides, again biplanes but less elderly. Seats could be tricky to reserve on the early-morning flight to St Mary's; Messrs Treglown, the Penzance booking agents, sometimes denied it existed, anxious to keep places vacant in case of urgently-required tradesmen and other skilled folk. However, either airfield would also take reservations, the quaint telephone numbers (St Just 60 or 79, and Scillonia 46) reflecting the truly rural environment. By 1957, ticket prices were £1.10s (£1.50) single and £2.10s (£2.50) return. At St Mary's, the old airport bus was available for the short trip into Hugh Town, though some felt it was almost quicker to walk. The route was said to be BEA's busiest internal flight, making over twenty round trips a day during the high-season. By 1958, three faithful Rapides were still in use: G-AHKU Cecil John Rhodes, G-AHLL Sir Henry Lawrence and G-AKZB Lord Baden-Powell.

But finally, in August 1963 BEA ordered a modern Sikorsky S-61N helicopter for its Scilly service. The aging Rapides needed ever-increasing support and their pilots were becoming fewer, while the S-61 could carry three times the passengers. BEA felt the operating limitations at St Mary's particularly would favour the helicopter rather than a fixed-wing replacement; the Rapides had been retained

▲ **De Havilland DH.89A Rapide** G-AKZB Lord Baden Powell, seen at Land's End while serving on BEA's route to St Mary's during the 1950s. In 1961, 'KZB crashed at Land's End in fog, but no one was hurt (Author's Collection).

for so long chiefly because they were hard to replace in terms of fixed-wing aircraft. The S-61, G-ASNL, flew its first scheduled service between Land's End and St Mary's on 2 May 1964, and the Rapides were sold off to Exeter-based British Westpoint Airlines. In September, BEA opened a new heliport at Eastern Green, Penzance, just west of the field from where Claude Grahame-White had performed his historic flight in July 1910, and the mainland helicopter service moved from Land's End.

Over the previous few years, meanwhile, civil air traffic at RAF St Mawgan had gradually grown. During early 1962, talks had been held between Newquay Council and the Air Ministry. The Ministry had agreed to the Council's proposals; part of St Mawgan was set aside, becoming known as Newquay Airport (RAF St Mawgan), and a small civil terminal building was built. In April, Westpoint Aviation (as the company had then been known) started a scheduled passenger service flying a Douglas DC-3 between Newquay, Exeter and Heathrow. Mayflower Air Services also flew from the new airport, using Rapides, but after a serious accident in July 1963 the concern faded away.

The 1965 summer season saw the introduction of the first flights by British Midland Airways between Newquay and Castle Donington, again with DC-3s. By the following summer British Eagle Airways was flying BAC 1-11s on its

▲ **End of an** era. Replacing the Rapides, BEA's first S-61N helicopter on the Land's End – St Mary's route was G-ASNL Orion, photographed here at the St Mary's terminus over the summer of 1963 (AUTHOR'S COLLECTION).

Newquay route, the first commercial jets to operate there, and that service was resumed for the summer of 1967. In the meantime, the Rapides had refused to go into retirement, instead being used by Scillonia Airways for services between Newquay, Land's End and St Mary's until 1969, when the concern was liquidated. That year too, budget airline Dan-Air commenced a Gatwick – Newquay passenger service.

৩৵৶

For military aviation in Cornwall, the immediate post-war period was a mixed bag. By 1948 both Predannack and St Mawgan had closed, but St Merryn and St Eval continued. St Merryn carried on with its naval training role, the work generally routine but during July 1947, a Seafire of 736 Squadron force-landed off Padstow following rocket-firing practice at Treligga. The pilot stayed with the aircraft to prevent it crashing into the town's crowded streets, and it broke up in the soft sand of the Camel estuary. St Eval was retained as the main Coastal Command station in the area and in January 1947 203 Squadron arrived, converting from Liberators to Lancasters.

Three months later, a new Cornish airfield was commissioned. Its planning had begun during the war years and the new station opened for business on 17 April 1947, named RNAS Culdrose (HMS Seahawk). The first unit at Culdrose was 780 Squadron of the Naval Instrument Flying Instructional Flight, flying Oxfords and Harvards, which arrived to begin an instrument training role. During January 1948, 792 Squadron, at St Merryn during the war, reformed at Culdrose as a Night Fighter Training Unit using Fireflies, Oxfords, and three Ansons fitted with airborne interception radar. In March the School of Naval Air Warfare moved from St Merryn to Culdrose, and during February 1950 736 Squadron also arrived, bringing some fifty Sea Fury fighters.

In November 1951 the first Shackleton four-engined maritime patrol aircraft appeared in Cornwall, when 220 Squadron moved to St Eval. They were followed by 42 Squadron during June 1952 and 206 Squadron in September, also flying Shackletons. By that summer, St Eval was one of twelve Master Diversion Airfields in the UK, open 365 days a year around the clock, for use by aircraft diverted because of bad weather or emergency. When its Lancasters left the station in the latter part of 1952, St Eval became all-Shackleton except for the Station Flight's Walrus, Tiger Moth, Oxford and Martinet.

▲ **July 1968: Vickers Viscount** airliner G-AWCV of British Midlands Airways at Newquay airport. At the top of the steps, the air-stewardess waits to greet the passengers. In the background are St Mawgan's RAF installations (Barry Cole).

On 16 April 1951 the decision was made to re-open St Mawgan, for use by the School of Maritime Reconnaissance and their Lancasters. New accommodation huts appeared to the rear of the control tower, supplementing the wartime buildings. The School's jobs were to improve anti-submarine warfare skills in the light of experiences during the Korean War, and teach the techniques needed to operate the Shackleton in that role. Shortly after the School began work, the Air Sea Warfare Development Unit also arrived, housed at the Trebelzue end of the station. Again the ASWDU flew Shackletons, with the task of conducting trials on newly-developed equipment and creating procedures for its use. From those beginnings, St Mawgan went on to remain a maritime air base until the 1990s.

By 1953 St Merryn housed the School of Aircraft Maintenance, and the Naval Air Ordnance School also arrived. However, as the Fleet Air Arm focused increasingly on Culdrose, for St Merryn the writing on the wall became clear. Its runways, adequate by wartime standards, were viewed as short by the mid-fifties, and in June 1955 the airfield was reduced to Care and Maintenance. On 10 January 1956 St Merryn was closed by the Royal Navy.

▲ **During the 1950s** RNAS Culdrose was home to many fixed-wing Squadrons, mostly training units. Here is Fairey Firefly T.2 DK527 of 765 Squadron, a tactical weapons trainer, seen at the station during 1955 (PETER WEARNE).

During the fifties, Culdrose continued to grow as a flying training station. In early 1950 No 1 Naval Air Fighter School was established, and August saw the formation of the Advanced Jet Flying School, using Attackers and Meteors. During October 1951, 778 Squadron began Airborne Early Warning trials from Culdrose using adapted Skyraider aircraft carrying radar in a ventral dome. The trials were successful, providing radar coverage over around a hundred miles to help protect British fleets from attack; 778 became the nucleus of 849 Squadron, which began a long association with Culdrose. During July 1955, Culdrose's first Fairey Gannet anti-submarine squadron was formed when 825 Squadron was recommissioned.

In November 1956, 228 Squadron's Shackletons moved from St Eval to St Mawgan, followed in December by 220 Squadron; these were St Mawgan's first operational squadrons. 220 flew the new Shackleton MR.3, which was too heavy to take off from St Eval and needed the longer runways of St Mawgan. During January 1958, 206 Squadron also transferred to St Mawgan, as a second Shackleton MR.3 squadron. With the transfer of these operations to St Mawgan, during March 1959 St Eval was reduced to Care and Maintenance status.

During May 1958, the Navy's Electronic Warfare Unit reformed as 831 Squadron at Culdrose using Avengers and later Gannets, but also retained its Sea Venom 21 (ECM) jets, based at the station between shipboard exercises. During 1959 the School of Aircraft Handling also arrived, created to provide instruction in manoeuvring aircraft on carrier flight-decks. As the decade came to an end, the Navy chose Culdrose as its main training base for the introduction of helicopters into service. In January 1958, 705 Squadron arrived, bringing their Whirlwind and Dragonfly rotorcraft.

In June 1959, 700H Squadron formed the Intensive Flying Trials Unit for the introduction of the new Whirlwind HAS.7 helicopter at Culdrose, while August saw 700G Squadron form the IFTU for the Gannet AEW.3 airborne early warning aircraft. The IFTUs' tasks were to develop handling techniques and solve engineering problems with new types, as well as to train crews for operational flying. April 1960 saw the arrival of the reformed 700H Squadron, the IFTU for the Wessex HAS.1 anti-submarine helicopter. Toward the end of the 1960s, the Navy began the introduction of the large Sea King helicopter. 700S (IFTU) Squadron received Sea King HAS.1s at Culdrose for trials, and over forty years on, many examples of the later marks are still based at the station.

At St Mawgan, the Shackletons continued their maritime patrol work as well as carrying out a number of overseas trips, but in March 1965 201 Squadron left for Kinloss in Scotland, joined that July by 206 Squadron. In exchange,

▲ **Avro Shackletons flew** widely from Cornwall, from November 1951 until the arrival of the Nimrod. Photographed over the Cornish coast during September 1967 is a T.4 version, WB822, flown by the Maritime Operational Training Unit based at St Mawgan (Chris Ashworth).

St Mawgan received the Shackleton T.4s of the Maritime Operational Training Unit, providing conversion training from the early Shackletons to the more sophisticated MR.3 version.

On 28 June 1968, the first production Nimrod MR.1 maritime patrol aircraft made its first flight from Hawker Siddeley's Woodford factory airfield. The Nimrod had been developed from the Comet passenger jet to replace the Shackleton, and during October 1969 236 Operational Conversion Unit received its first examples at St Mawgan, its job to transfer Shackleton crews to the new type.

During June 1972 the small passenger airline Brymon began a scheduled route between Newquay Airport and St Mary's using Britten-Norman Islander aircraft, twin-engined workhorses carrying eight to ten passengers. The following year Brymon opened a new service linking St Mary's with Exeter. In 1974, twenty-seat de Havilland Canada DHC.6 Twin Otters were introduced to the company's routes, and during January 1977 Brymon took over the running of Newquay Airport. As the seventies drew to an end, Viscount airliner operations also grew at Newquay; Alidair, Guernsey Air Lines and Jersey European Air Lines all ran services.

▲ **Brymon's DHC.6 Twin** Otter G-BFGP makes a visit to the grass of Bodmin during July 1979, one of the airfield's largest ever visitors. Behind the aeroplane are the tops of Bodmin's hangars, located in a dip (CHRIS ASHWORTH).

Over the following years, Brymon went on to acquire a fleet of de Havilland Canada Dash 7 turboprop regional airliners, and later Dash 8s. By the spring of 1985, its Scilly connections ran to Bristol, Exeter, Newquay and Plymouth, and Brymon continued those services until it was acquired by British Airways in 1993.

During March 1994 a spacious new terminal was opened at Newquay Airport, backed financially by Cornwall County Council and Restormel Borough Council. Today, Air Southwest, Flybe, Ryanair, Jet 2, Skybus, Lufthansa and BMI Baby all fly from the re-named Newquay Cornwall Airport; Air Southwest is currently up for sale.

Since September 1972, the Penzance - St Mary's route had been run by British Airways Helicopters (BAH), successor to BEA Helicopters. In October 1974, S-61N helicopter G-BCEB had arrived, fitted with luggage lockers beneath its passenger cabin at the expense of reduced fuel tankage; no problem on the short hops to and from St Mary's. An additional BAH service was introduced in March 1983 when the Penzance – Tresco route via St Mary's was opened. A further change in ownership followed; in September 1985 the company was renamed British International Helicopters, its proprietor Robert Maxwell. Today, it trades as British International Helicopter Services, and old faithful G-BCEB still toils back and forth across West Penwith's skies, its internal layout occasionally altered to include a dog crate at the expense of two of its usual cabin seats. The route is the longest-established regular helicopter service in the world. Currently though, British International plans to move the mainland end of its operation from Penzance Heliport to Land's End airfield.

During the spring of 1984, meanwhile, the Isles of Scilly Steamship Company had applied to operate daily scheduled flights between Land's End and St Mary's. It was March 1987 before permission was granted, and the ISSC's aerial subsidiary, named Skybus, began a service using Islanders, including the appropriately-registered G-SBUS. For the 1991/1992 season, Skybus launched flights from Exeter; during the following year a Newquay – Plymouth service began, followed by links to Bristol in 1994 and Southampton in 1997. Although the company is best known for its Scilly service, it has provided charter trips to a variety of destinations including Cork, the Channel Islands, London Heathrow, Brittany and the French Alps, taking a ski party from Newquay. During 2008, flights were launched to Cardiff, and St Brieuc in Brittany; in 2009 the St Brieuc route continued.

The journey between Land's End and St Mary's takes about fifteen minutes at around 1,500 ft, not much quicker than in 1937; service is relaxed and friendly. On the busiest Saturdays of the holiday season, Skybus makes as many as forty-five round trips. Land's End has a miniature but comfortable terminal,

▲ **Isles of Scilly** Skybus Islander bearing the nifty identity G-SSKY, at rest at Land's End during the mid-1990s. In the background is the airfield's control tower (AUTHOR).

along with a sun terrace from where the aircraft can be viewed. Big brothers to the Islander fleet are the company's Twin Otters, generally used on the longer-haul routes. From a servicing point of view the piston-engined Islanders are more suited for many very short journeys than the turbine-powered Twin Otters. Currently, Skybus operates three of each type.

ഗര

During May 1970, 7 Squadron reformed at RAF St Mawgan on Canberra TT.18 target-tug jets, towing targets for Army and Navy units nationwide. The Squadron also provided aircraft acting as low and fast targets, to allow radar and unloaded surface-to-air weapons to practice their tracking skills. In April 1971, 42 Squadron began converting to Nimrod MR.1s at St Mawgan for anti-submarine warfare, surveillance of Warsaw Pact naval forces, and search and rescue work, as well as fishery protection and oil-rig surveillance duties. Once the crews had been trained, St Mawgan's Nimrods were pooled between 42 Squadron and 236 OCU, and centralised servicing was adopted.

During the Fastnet Race tragedy of 1979, 42 Squadron had three aircraft airborne at a time on search and rescue missions. In mid-January 1981, a 42 Squadron Nimrod participated in the rescue of a Dutch Air Force crew after their Breguet Atlantic maritime patrol aircraft crashed west of Ireland. To search for survivors, the Nimrod conducted visual sweeps only three hundred feet above the waves; that day, nine lives were saved. A contrasting episode involved a radio conversation which allegedly took place between a patrolling 42 Squadron Nimrod and an inexperienced yacht skipper in distress. Nimrod: "What is your position?" Yacht skipper: "I am the Managing Director of a shoe manufacturing company."

May 1982 saw St Mawgan involved in Operation Corporate, when 42 Squadron Nimrods departed for Ascension Island for surface surveillance and anti-submarine support duties during the Falklands war. By then, most of the Squadron's aircraft had received new hemp camouflage at the expense of their former grey and white scheme. During 1984 both 236 OCU and 42 Squadron converted to the Nimrod MR.2 version, which employed a radically-updated electronics fit. In 1988 St Mawgan's main runway was completely resurfaced, but the 1990s saw the departure of the Nimrods, the last of which left for Kinloss on 9 September 1992.

During 2005, St Mawgan was one of the bases shortlisted to house the forthcoming Joint Combat Aircraft fighter from 2013. However, late that year it was announced by the Armed Forces Minister, Adam Ingram, that the work would go to RAF Lossiemouth instead. During 2008, RAF flying at St Mawgan ended.

But in contrast with the military fortunes of St Mawgan, Culdrose has blossomed. During the early seventies its accommodation and recreational facilities were expanded, while nearby, the old RAF Predannack was revived as an additional training facility and given a new control tower. Culdrose and Predannack now cover a combined area of over 1,500 acres.

Culdrose's Sea King helicopters have been involved in scores of rescue missions around the Cornish coast and beyond, some straightforward, others tremendously difficult. On 16 January 1974 the Danish coaster Merc Enterprise signalled Mayday off Plymouth, in near gale-force weather. Five Sea Kings hurried to the scene, including two Federal German examples at Culdrose for training. They found the upturned keel of the vessel and its crew in the water. Despite wretched conditions the helicopters rescued several survivors at great personal risk, not least to their winchmen who were repeatedly immersed in freezing seas. Eleven of the nineteen crew were saved, the Sea Kings working with various surface vessels which had also arrived to help. Two of the helicopters

▲ **The RAF flew** Nimrod maritime patrol aircraft from RAF St Mawgan between October 1969 and September 1992. Here is XV246 in the later hemp camouflage, coming in to land (BARRY COLE).

▲ **A rotary trio** from RNAS Culdrose, caught over the Cornish coastline during the mid-1970s. Nearest, Gazelle trainer XW868 of 705 Squadron; middle, 771 Squadron's Wessex rescue helicopter XS873; and 826 Squadron's Sea King HAS.1 XV647 anti-submarine helicopter (RNAS CULDROSE).

were eventually obliged to return to land, their engines malfunctioning due to spray and salt ingestion; both made crash-landings on the Lizard. The Merc Enterprise rescue operation resulted in the award of two Air Force Crosses and three Air Force Medals to the Sea King airmen.

For many years, the Sea King was the main strength at Culdrose. In May 1982, 825 Squadron reformed there as a trooping and heavy lift squadron on the Sea King HAS.2A, for service with the Falklands Task Force. During that month, eight aircraft embarked in the Atlantic Causeway, and two in the Queen Elizabeth II. In the following month a detachment was put ashore at Port San Carlos. That memorable summer too, a record twenty-eight thousand people attended the Culdrose Air Day.

849 Squadron acquired the Sea King airborne early warning helicopter, fitted with Thorn EMI Searchwater maritime surveillance radar in an air-pressurised Kevlar thimble dome projecting from the starboard side. The Sea Kings of 810 Squadron were used for anti-submarine warfare training, and from 1993, 814, 820 and 849 Sea King Squadrons all took part in the NATO and later Implementation Force operations off Bosnia, carrying out surface search, search-and-rescue, load-lifting and personnel transfer tasks.

771 Squadron still flies red and grey-painted Sea Kings, providing search and rescue facilities for military and civilian purposes, every day of the year, round the clock, within a radius of two hundred nautical miles from Culdrose. The aircraft are at fifteen minutes' notice by day and forty-five by night, though they are usually much quicker to respond. On average, the squadron carries out well over two hundred missions a year, and is also involved in pollution control, aircrew training and troop lifting.

▲ **A rare Polish** PZL-Bielsko SZD-45A Ogar (Hound) powered glider, G-OGAR, spied taxying in the summer sun at Perranporth airfield during 2009 (AUTHOR).

Today too, Culdrose is the largest single-site employer in Cornwall and the Royal Navy's biggest shore establishment; on a busy day it carries out as many aircraft movements as a major international airport. To its helicopter strength has been added the new Merlin HM.1, flown by 814 and 829 anti-submarine warfare Squadrons, and by 824 Squadron in a training role. Often seen over the Duchy too are the blue-and-white Jetstream aircraft of 750 Squadron, the station's observer training unit.

On the lighter side of Cornish civil aviation, several small airfields are currently operating, their private aircraft particularly active at the weekends. At Cardinham, near Bodmin, an airfield was established on the flat moorland during the early seventies by Mike Robertson, founder of the Trago Mills retail empire; in 1972 he set up the Cornwall Flying Club there. From its original clutch of Forney F-1As, Ercoupes and Aircoupes, at present the club flies two Cessna 152s, a Cessna 172 and a Robin 2160 using its two grass runways.

Since 1980, the old RAF Davidstow station has been home to the microlights of the Moorland Flying Club, one of the first such groups in the country. Davidstow Airfield and Cornwall at War Museum, located in refurbished wartime airfield buildings, covers a wide history of local aviation as well as other military themes; pride of place in its collection goes to a rare 1956 ex-Royal Navy Fairey Gannet electronic countermeasures aircraft.

Perranporth airfield hosts the Cornish Gliding (and Flying) Club at its northern end and though at present the group is inactive, there are plans to remedy that. The southern part accommodates Perranporth Flying Club, which has over a hundred members, some training for their pilot's licences and others who fly their own aircraft; also available are scenic flights and parachuting. The wartime watch-tower has been renovated for use by the club. With its old fighter dispersal pens, pillboxes and other remaining RAF structures, the site is one of the best preserved Second World War fighter stations in Britain, and has been designated a scheduled monument by English Heritage. Close by the airfield runs the beautiful Cornwall Coast Path; on a sunny afternoon why not go for a clifftop stroll, a gentle wander? Vivid purple heathers and golden gorse, the blue twinkly sea, maybe some sandwiches along the way and while you're walking, a free air-show – enjoy!

Acknowledgements

I'm delighted to acknowledge the kind generosity and practical support I've received from the following people and organisations over the years, which has allowed me to produce *Flying In Cornwall*.

The late Chris Ashworth, Tim Bishop, Paddy Bradley, Denys Bryant, the late Barry Cole, Cornish Studies Library, Neville Doyle, Rod Knight, Stuart Leslie, Malcolm McCarthy, the late Ces Mowthorpe, RNAS Culdrose, Royal Canadian Air Force, Royal Cornwall Polytechnic Research Project, Hugh Sheridan, Andrew Thomas, Reg Watkiss, Peter Wearne, Bill Young.

All reasonable measures have been taken to identify correctly the sources of the images used in this book. If use has accidentally been made without correct acknowledgement of the originator, please accept my apologies. Should such a situation arise and the publisher is notified accordingly, I would be pleased to make a suitable amendment for inclusion in any future editions of this book.